Awareness: Being Fully Alive

Heart to Heart is Where We Start

by

Robert S. Cosmar

Du Bois PA

Magic Man's Universe Publishing
aka Barking Spiders Publishing

ISBN# 978-0-9839320-7-9

Awareness
Copyright 2011 Robert S. Cosmar

All Rights Reserved
First Printing -- 2011

Requests for information or interviews
should be addressed to:

Robert S. Cosmar
% Magic Man's Universe
705 W. Long Ave
Du Bois, PA 15801
814-591-3363

Other Books by Robert S. Cosmar:
Trilogy of Awareness 2011

Printed in USA
Magic Man's Universe Publishing
aka Barking Spiders Publishing

Choices

Life is full of crossroads,
hard lefts and harder rights
with other paths and curves
going this way or that.
Each way has its own
set of bumps, and the
occasional hairpin turn.
Choices are new chances
to learn and grow
and gain more awareness.
We're never alone,
if we open our heart
our guidance whispers ...
Dusting myself off,
I've wondered at times
how my life might have
differed, had I taken
a different route.
Lord knows, I could have
used a few more straight
stretches along the way,
but at least I made choices,
some good, some not so good,
but each was perfect for me
at the time, creating
the being that now is.
How sad for those
who merely hitchhike
through life never daring
to choose at all.

by C.J. Heck

3

This book is dedicated to the love of my life,

Cathy Parrish (C. J. Heck),

whose support, dedication, encouragement and

editing have made all my works possible.

Introduction

Life is what you are aware of. If you are only aware of labels, opinions and the ideas of others, then you are not truly alive. You are merely a copy following another copy and they've probably followed yet another copy.

Existence has made you unique, but over the years, social programming has made you less than that and pain and suffering are the result.

This book is a collection of essays I wrote over a period of several months in 2010. They are about awareness and touch a deep sensitivity in all of us. They ask you to do more than think. They beg you to *feel* and then to turn those feelings inside and follow them. It is a privilege to share them now with you.

Sincerely,

Robert S. Cosmar

Table of Contents

Awareness Follows Attention

Awareness: the ability to see with knowingness. It is pure consciousness, without identification. Awareness is the essence of what we are within. Looking outside ourselves from a point of conscious awareness within, we need language to explain, explore, and understand existence in its physical sense.

Mind: awareness *without* knowingness of reality. It is perception without the knowingness of consciousness or reality. Mind, therefore, is anti-knowingness. We do not *know* with the mind; we only label, analyze and arrange concepts in logical order. We try to express knowingness in language, which is only a symbol of our conscious knowing, but this is not what we actually know or perceive. Mind is a container that holds ideas, memories, and unconscious content.

When the attention is turned within, through feelings and not thoughts, we perceive that knowingness exists. This knowingness exists beyond and without words. It is experiences as a unity of thought and being. We realize it is the truth of our being, or a level of conscious realization, well beyond the mind, and part of something deeper and richer within.

Awareness is how we perceive reality, in both the inner and outer worlds. Attention is how we choose to give direction to consciousness, so awareness can respond with understanding.

We are complete, just as we are, but the division of our attention can cause a split in awareness. This can cause great confusion. It is only when our attention is seated deep within, and our awareness grounded in the core of our being, that we are able to understand and accept reality "as is". This is *home*, our true face, and our total being of consciousness

Success is not Success Without Awareness

Success is not success, unless you are happy, and happiness is not possible without awareness. Awareness assures you that your achievement is in alignment with your evolution and the purposes of existence. People are allowed to achieve great things in this world, but many lack the awareness to hold onto it. Life denies us nothing, but it does expect us to learn the real meaning of success.

Awareness shows us that no matter what you accumulate in life, it will all pass. Yes, you can pass it along to your kids or relatives, but you still have to let go of it. You can't take it with you, because you don't know how or where that is.

Life appears to end when we leave this sandbox called earth. We have learned to cultivate, mine and exploit all kinds of wealth in this world, except the wealth of the heart and soul. We have further failed to exchange this rich wealth with other cultures and races. We have become separate and isolated by our imbalance of wealth. We make monsters of the wealthy through jealousy and we damn the poor as ignorant and unworthy of wealth. All these judgments are one-sided and biased by our limited perceptions.

When we are aware, we know through wisdom what the proper course of action is. We know what is just, proper and right for us. We understand what existence is allowing us to achieve. We do not seek what is beyond the means of our awareness. We understand our place and accept it. The wealth of our awareness is far more precious than all our material gain or achievements. We don't want it all, because we already have it all.

Nothing is Ever Wasted

Years ago, when I was in Denver, I had the privilege of experiencing what, at the time, amazed me. I had met a woman from back east and we became quick friends. She was in Denver escaping a bad marriage and I was seeking my own path of self-expression and discovery.

She, as it turned out, was a deep trance channel and, after a slow start, we began to converse with her spirit guide. She could both trance channel him and also hear him. We spent several months having groups come to her house where her guide would enter her body and talk to us about our lives, the world, and why we were here. It was all very magical and fascinating.

Months after the sessions stopped and we had all gone our separate ways, my friend was instructed by her spirit guide to write down the content of those sessions. It was interesting to see the documentation which was nearly two inches thick. She had copied verbatim from the tapes to paper, making two copies, one for me and one for her. I didn't realize we had talked so much!

What followed next was amazing, because I did not expect it. I couldn't understand how the universe could embed what it did into those random meetings. She and I sat one afternoon with our copies, while her guide had us highlight areas of the manuscript that were supposed to become seminars for others. It almost made me laugh, because elegantly and spontaneously, order had been created out of what seemed to be random chaos.

The seminar topics were designed to be shared with those interested in reviving their inner child. Companies as well

15

as other people could re-create wonder and excitement to provide alternate possibilities for lives that had become rigid and dry. It's unfortunate that those seminars never manifested -- the power in them was extraordinary and rejuvenating. It would have been fun and, I'm sure, successful for those brave enough to allow their inner child to be reborn.

Gift of Awareness

Awareness is the greatest of all gifts. It is free to share, when appropriate, and it's never manipulative or controlling, and harmonizes two hearts into agreement. It is the division of existence through the mind that creates turmoil and pain. Life is seen in parts and divided by judgments about the nature of reality. We are forced to choose and so limited in our ability to see comprehensively all sides of a situation. We become blind, prejudiced and divided.

Awareness is the gift of seeing totally from a higher perspective within us. It comes as a knowing and not a series of propositions, arguments or theories. We know and we are certain we know, but we may not know how it is that we know. Awareness equalizes the field and applies understanding to our minds and hearts.

Peace is a gift and byproduct of awareness. Conflict is ended and harmony is restored to us and others. It is the lack of awareness that prevents the world and its people from coming together. Awareness reveals that there is but one world, one universe, one people and one truth. This truth is not of religion or God, but of a personal connection to it through consciousness. You do not *learn* awareness. It arises out of the conflict of mind and heart and is often born in turmoil.

Awareness is the true gift of life, the energy of the eternal flowing from one heart to another and healing the separations of race, creed and color. It is tasting our true identity and remembering the greatest good within us. Dare to be aware and then dare to share it.

How to Look Within

Most people are perplexed when you tell them they must look within. The mind asks how can you do that? It even seems ridiculous to try, but when you realize that inner looking is actually *feeling*, it is a different matter all together.

The mind explores through thought, memory and observation. It analyzes what it hears, sees and thinks. It takes concepts and arranges them, according to its understanding. Feelings are centered in the heart and have deep connections leading to the very source of life itself -- the soul of existence.

Feeling is an internally directed process and not external, like thought is. Feelings require no observation, other than to be aware of them, or to turn your attention to them. No work or analysis is needed -- you just *feel*. The hard part is trusting those feelings and learning how they reveal so much of the mystery of life and ourselves.

Feelings help us to understand the mystery of life and ourselves by revealing to us our unity with life. Unlike the mind, the feelings reveal what is already there and how we are a part of it. Understanding is not required. You don't have to come to any conclusions, you simply know.

Silence is a byproduct of deep feeling. As the mind stops its chatter, you become aware of a vacuum or void in which only a solitary *you* exists.

At first, this void has elements of the unconscious you in it, but as you go deeper and encounter the blocks to full realization, you come to understand the meaning and importance of silence. Silence reveals what words cannot. It is a place where concepts are replaced by reality and the end of seeking is because you have found the essence of life and your place within it.

Silence requires no time or space to define it, because in the inner world of reality, it is the companion of reality. It dissolves the illusions created in time and space and brings us to a point of realization where we see, through feeling, the nature of ourselves and true reality. We are home again and we know it. We remember and recognize it all ... the search is over, at least for now.

To Make a Difference

When I was growing up, there were certain movies that seemed to touch me deeply. Sometimes I would cry, and at other times, my heart would just swell within me. It seemed that the movies which affected me most involved either an underdog overcoming a bully or evil person, or movies about Jesus touching a person's life, such as Ben Hur. Till recently I did not realize why I cried.

I was sitting on the couch with Cathy during the last few days, and we watched a couple of movies that made me cry. One was the new Karate Kid. The other movie was an older movie called Mona Lisa Smile. Both movies were either about helping people overcome an obstacle, or to realize their full potential.

I came to see in these movies that most of my life, my greatest desire was either to realize my own full potential or to help others achieve theirs. I was crying for myself and for others, as well.

I have had moments in my life when I felt the hand of God, or providence, touch me and I realized how important that was. There are also times when I realized I touched peoples' lives as well, and I always remember that feeling of getting through to them.

Nothing feels better then a breakthrough moment when after years maybe of miscommunication, or even misunderstanding a person or persons, then finally SEE and a doorway to life is opened and you or they overcome an obstacle or realize a long held dream. You feel happy for them and grateful that you had a part in in helping them.

Accept Yourself

Most people do not like their personal *self*. Many more do not know *self*. We live in a mental world full of ideas, thoughts, and opinions. Our identities are borrowed, from society, our parents, even our peers. Only when our goals, dreams and desires collapse before us do we consider that life is not what we have been told or sold. We suffer when this happens, but the suffering is a birth, of sorts, and an opportunity to rediscover our true *self* and its power.

Fear and distrust of self prevent most people from coming to terms with who they are. The world applies pressure for them to conform to the norm or suffer the fate of being dubbed a failure. What they are being told is, "Who we want you to be is more important than who you feel you are." What we have, therefore, are highly educated failures as human beings -- people who can talk and think, for sure, but who lack an awareness of self and how they fit into the universal scheme of things. It is one thing to identify with a thing or a philosophy yet entirely another to know the self as an individual. One encourages conformity, the other causes us to go on a personal journey within to find our true and unique self.

Until the mind and heart are again merged into a cosmic partnership with the knowing heart as the lead guide, mankind will continue to fail in its attempt to achieve purpose. Mankind will not be able to conquer outer space until we have achieved a greater awareness of our inner space. Man can only achieve great things in proportion to his ability to understand himself. It is awareness that has brought the discovery of great achievements in our time and many of those are outside the realm of thought.

Before you begin to find yourself, you have to look within. Before you begin to contemplate about who you think you are, you have to look at the way you *feel* you are. Nothing is more damaging to a soul than a runaway mind seeking itself through thoughts, and a person hiding or evading how they feel. You are not just your thoughts. Your feelings are much deeper and truer to your natural being or self.

Do not judge yourself or anyone else, based on what you see or think -- open your heart and accept them. Some will be your teachers and help you to learn about yourself. Others will be a reminder of your own prejudices and vices -- no one is better than anyone else. Until we see deeply into our self, we will not have the power to achieve our dreams in a manner that reflects our true identity.

Trust

If we don't have trust in ourselves, in life, and in others, then we feel cut off and abandoned. That kind of life is against our needs, hopes and desires. I'm not talking about common trust, but something much deeper.

Basic and fundamental trust in the integrity of our connection in consciousness is imperative to all that IS. This is a knowing, that we are a part of the universal whole. Most of us have limited trust or maybe a trust with conditions, but this kind of trust will not weather a storm of doubt or apparent betrayal. It does not see deeply enough or far enough into the purposes of the magic.

Total, absolute trust or surrender is the way we melt into our deepest nature, the magic or the love. At some point in our lives, we all need to open ourselves, trust and share our common humanness and realize we are all the same. We may look different, sound different or feel different, but human needs, desires, wants and our problems are all universal.

To trust is to risk rejection on many levels, but it's also the only way to a deeper love of self and others. It is the glue that binds us all and supports our common need for love. The world and your life are seen from a different place when you view them with an open heart that trusts.

The Art of Waiting

It is so frustrating, having to wait. We wait for our dreams to manifest; we wait for a direction to take; we wait for an inspiration to write. It doesn't seem fair to have to wait, and it brings up aspects of ourselves that are not always pretty. We like having control over our lives and having *what* we want, *when* we want it. Yet if we don't learn patience, the impatience can blossom into a demanding and stubborn state of mind.

Good things do happen when we are ready for them and, when it's time, they manifest effortlessly. No inner struggle is needed, it just happens, and we're grateful for it. However, the mind and ego are never satisfied. Selfishly oriented, they seek to fulfill themselves immediately and give little consideration to others, their needs, or the wisdom of timing. Actually, part of the problem is this idea of time. Our egos and minds are taught to obsess over time and dwell on it as if our lives were all about time. Time is how people conduct the business of living, but time is not living.

Surrender to what is -- this is necessary to overcome the threat of time. Acceptance of what is, is also necessary. A realization that everything is happening perfectly, just as it should be, is the cure for waiting -- and it's the only cure. The mind and time never give answers, only demands. They are never your best friends in life, but necessary tools in which to live and maneuver through our daily living.

There's an old saying that people use: "You'll understand in time"; however, this is only true for those who become aware that everything happens for a reason and when it is supposed to. Nothing happens by chance.

Love is eternally patient because it knows it will get the desire of its heart eventually. It may take a thousand years, but it will achieve its desire. Time exists to give the illusion that somehow we have a right or destiny to control things and make them happen when we want. Nothing could be further from the truth.

Unless you are surrendered and aware, the opportunities and gifts hidden in delays or waiting are never seen. This puts the heart in danger of shutting down. In the end, it isn't a matter of getting what we want, when we want it, but rather what we have become and realized. Are we more aware? Or rather, are we more bitter, as a result of our limited ability to have things our way?

Only the heart knows ... what does yours say to you right now?

The Magic of Feeling

Forget all the things you have been told about religion, mysticism, occult knowledge, psychology, philosophy and power. They are all like eating a picture of a steak dinner from a magazine page and believing it will fill you up.

Feel, just feel! Feel your life and feel *how* you feel and *what* you feel. This is life. This is what is real. This is the gateway to the real you. Feel the way to the eternal you. Yearn for it and ask for it. The mind is for this world, but the heart and feelings are for all worlds.

Simplicity! Nothing is complex, so don't think it to death. Just feel! Feel the waves of depth within you. Feel the fear, the hope and the love. Feelings speak from deep within. Feelings tell us how to escape the trap of sin.

You can search the mind all you want, but it can't answer the question of life. Life is not an idea -- it is, it simply is. You can feel life and you can embrace it with your heart. Speak to it in your despair. Touch it with your tears. Know life in your heart.

If you will only feel, soon life will reveal to you what is truly real.

Write When it is Time

There is a time to write and there is a time to rest from it. A cycle of creative expression exists in all things and has to be accepted. It is very rare that anyone does not have to stop and realize the time of writing has stopped or is over for now. It would be great to continually express our feelings and thoughts as they pour through us, but then when would we have time to learn and reflect about all that we have written? The dry times, the time's when we feel we have hit a wall are those approaches to the next layer of our preparation to know ourselves more deeply and honestly.

Writing is mostly self revelation and self confession. We write what we realize through creative channels and we wait to write about our pain as we discover that we are not a complete person yet.

Fear, limitation, frustration and depression continually confront us on our journey to wholeness. These limits to our free expression are the barriers to our true knowledge of self. They hide our true identity, they hold us back. But they also reveal our excuses and reasons for failure to grow in awareness of ourselves and reality.

Until we are whole, this cycle of create and wait will always be there. Enjoy the flow of self as it passes through you and nourishes your heart. Then as the dry days come, accept them, and look at all the excuses, fears and blockages you have accepted to existence and yourself. The more that you relax and witness them, the sooner they can pass and reveal the next gift that they are bringing you.

Expression and Reflection

Life is a tide of outgoing expressions and incoming reflections. Daily we strive to serve the expressed wishes of someone else. Nightly we reflect on our lives and where we are or where we're going. Nothing is constant in time; all things change. This tide of experiences causes us to examine what we believe, think and want. It makes us examine our deepest desires and intentions. It asks us, "Are we true to our real nature?"

Your real nature is not divided or confused. It is clear, intent and compact. It knows its self intimately and deeply, with no enemies or detractors. It is linked to the chain of life and serves a purpose deep in the bosom of existence. It is a true marvel of our nature. We need this cycle of activity to learn about our self, our life and existence. It is through opposites that our real nature is exposed and we can choose to accept it, or not. In between the tide of expression and reflection is that thing we call *love*. Love is the true vibration emanating from our deepest core, and that is the essence behind the process of expression and reflection. All things evolve towards this center in time.

Love does not exist in time. Like most of our virtues, it is eternal and belongs to eternity and our real natures. In time, love and all true virtues are seldom seen or felt, because they are diminished by words, language and ideas. There is no true feeling of it, only an imitation of love spoken or stated. Not until man unites again the heart with the mind, will love be felt, spoken, and seen as true in time.

The tide of life exists so we can discover again our true

nature and express it eternally. It is our choice to accept or reject this -- no God stands in judgment to tell us what to do or what is right for us. It is our choice, as cells in the universal body, to decide whether we follow that which elevates us naturally or that which brings us harm. It is as simple as knowing how we feel and how our bodies react to what we are doing, deciding and choosing. We are never lost, just misguided and unconscious -- that is our only sin.

At times, the tide washes many surprises and precious gifts to the shore and it's important we don't resist. Enjoy your expression and also your reflection. In your moments of deepest despair are the seeds of your next exaltation.

We Make our own Bed

There is an old saying that "If you make your bed, you have to lie in it". This is true, in that there are consequences to our choices and decisions. Only in an absolute world would this be absolutely true, but this is not an absolute world, it's a relative one. Change occurs, evolution happens and we continue to realize our sacred cows are not so sacred after all. Choices are not eternal, and do not bind you forever. They can slow you down, stall your efforts and trap you in circles, but eventually there is a way out.

What would life be without death? For some, I'm sure, it's the only way to escape the choices they've made or the situation they're in. Part of the frustration of mankind is that rules, beliefs and speculations about existence all create barriers to reality. Real hope is only found in a transcendent realization of escape and freedom, not in human promises, beliefs or theories. You cannot be free of guilt if you believe in hell. You'll never be certain of salvation if you have to follow commandments. Only by knowing that you have the freedom to learn to be more aware through making unwise choices can you hope to evolve naturally and in partnership with existence.

Man has actually de-evolved to ideas about God and reality, because the mind rules. Someday, hopefully, the heart and feelings will reign again and man will again feel the long-dormant connection to existence. We are prisoners because we have rules, not because they are true.

Subject needs Object

Physical existence is not possible without a subject (creator) and an object (creation). Duality is the name of the game and it's how they relate that determines the manifestation we call life. Creation needs a force from which it manifests, an intelligence or a living consciousness that projects its will, purpose, plan or objective into existence. Creation cannot be by itself, it needs a source from which it manifests. Creator can exist alone, but then it is not expressing itself creatively. They must work together. They are interdependent on each other. They are also the same essence and must be a reflection reversely of each other.

Just as a camera inverts its image when taking a picture, creation must be empty of the essential qualities of the creator. In other words a creator must create in a vacuum. The reason is that it must provide a stage for creating that is empty of itself somehow, a place called anti-creator. You cannot put something into a box that is already full. The space has to be empty of mass, but it still has to include elements of the creator or its essence. Energy in some form must be available.

Humanity is both creator and created. At our core, we know who we are and why we are here -- all the answers are known to us, because we are that which exists. As the created, we exist in a vacuum which allows us to be separate from our creation. Our minds allow us to exist in a vacuum called *space and time* where we can forget our true selves and begin an endless journey back to it. Life is a journey outside the reality of who we are. This is why it is impossible to discover ourselves in space and time through our minds. However, it does allow us to explore our creative potential like a child in a sandbox. The sandbox is an imaginary playground, but when mom calls us for supper, we realize it is time to go inside our real home.

We and existence depend on a mirror reflection of both conscious and unconscious energy to manifest creation. We would not exist and the world or universe would not exist without it. It provides the stage within us where we forget ourselves and also remember ourselves, if we choose. It is infinite and spacious, never ending and easy to forget in it. To be hypnotized by our creations and forget as a child that it is not reality we are playing with, but a creation of our own imaginations.

To know yourself you must realize within yourself that you are both creation and creator and, even beyond that, you are essence of existence. What seems so far away and complex is in reality very simple and obvious in your awareness. It is the mind, searching through the millions of ideas, theories, and observations that is lost in itself and searching for something that does not exist as an object. Truth is never an object. It can be known and felt from within, but never discovered from without its nature.

A Grand Awakening

If humanity is to evolve and survive, then a grand event or awakening has to occur. It has to be strong enough that excuses from fear and ego pride have no place to run or the capacity to hide thru deceptions all too common to us in daily life. It has to be fearful enough to shake us from our sleep and make us realize we are responsible for all that we have created. This is the only hope and the only power that can save the path we have chosen till now.

Not until the wealthy, the famous, and royalty realize that greed not only steals from people but from a living universe will it all stop. Not until the poor and the ignorant stop blaming the rich and famous for their conditions in life and take responsibility for themselves will things change and both sides grow closer in wisdom and awareness.

Power is not real power, unless it is wrapped in awareness. Power that grows through manipulation, control and greed cannot be lasting. It has a seed of erosion and destruction within it. It creates jealousy and anger from those who feel powerless. It takes from others and leaves nothing behind of value for others to appreciate. Your power becomes an enemy to existence and to others. You are no longer seen as a flesh and blood person, but a vile worm of existence, eating the intestines of humanity. This is not the true purpose and intention of power.

Real power reveals the true nature of things and shows a unity of all existence. It teaches us that one power exists beyond the greed of humanity and, only when we surrender to it and the guidance of our hearts, do we have a chance to avoid destruction of ourselves and others. We are given the freedom to choose whether or not we will surrender to a greater wisdom that created it all or go our own way and see what happens. It is the hope of the heart of existence that we will all choose the way home to it, but the heart of existence will always permit us to leave and/or return forever.

The Fear of Truth

Nothing is more fearful than the truth. It peels away all misperception and lies. It unveils deceptions, both unintended and intentional. It lays us bear and naked to ourselves and often separates us from others as we gather ourselves and contemplate our next choices.

Everyone has had that moment of truth in a relationship where you thought you had something real and it manifested as a impostor. Nothing hurts so deeply or digs so painfully into us as when a moment of truth occurs. Discovering illusions is a death within us.

We think we know it all, and we are sure we have found it all. Nothing new can come or surprise us when life feels so good and we are sure it will last forever. Life and Love, however, have plans that go far beyond our perceptions and death, in its many forms, makes certain that the plan or love continues to flourish in time and space. This is why when you feel love and you have love, you have to appreciate it, because you never know when it might be taken away or will leave -- and it does. Time can be an opportunity to experience love, but there are no guarantees it will last or even exist beyond our current life.

It is a fear of truth that prevents love from growing, evolving, and blossoming. It is the compulsion to hold onto love too tightly, that strangles love and can make it die all too early. You have to risk love and realize its terms and conditions. The joy of getting can always turn into the pain of losing.

It is only through a living awareness that we understand and accept the plan of life. Sometimes we have a faint belief or intuition that it is not over -- it is never over. I will see you again is a stubborn hope that everyone echoes, but in reality, there is no promise of existence that it is so. Only through love and the feeling of what seems right can offer a hope of guarantee that we are eternally linked in a dance of existence together.

The more aware we become, the more of an individual we are. This realization can be confusing at first, as we feel our human need for love dissolving into a deepened love of self and others.

We can help each other to grow in love, to experience love, but in the end, it is our personal experience of it that really matters. The evolution of duality into the reality is the outcome of any enlightenment. This does not mean that we stop loving or caring. It simply means that emotional forms of love are replaced by a deeper more secure knowing of yourself and others. This allows more freedom and trust to express yourself and to create in partnership with existence.

We do move on through death and change, but the core of love in us all binds us into an eternal brother/sisterhood that never dies or changes. When we are really, finally at home within us, then and only then do we feel and recognize we are a cosmic family again

Nostalgia of Living

I am 60 years old and, over the past few years, I have looked into the past and reminisced over times, events and special memories of the years I have lived. I especially enjoy going to YouTube and seeing the 60's artists still singing their tunes from that time. It is both magical and sad, all at once. I am amazed at how those songs still ring deeply inside me and can arouse emotions and memories long buried. It is fun to watch the audience as they smile and recall their own memories, heartbreaks, and feelings.

I am also reminded that while it is good to relive the past, it is not good to be stuck there. Many people stay stuck in the past and never live a full life in the NOW. They have lived a long life and made choices that were unconscious. Time takes its toll on us mentally, emotionally and especially physically. Escaping to the past or having an addiction with the future seem like common ways to avoid the question, "What about NOW?" Death speaks louder with every friend or associate who leaves us, reminding us we are mortal and time is not our ally.

The years fly by and we sense an end is coming. All that we held familiar is slowly slipping from the hands of our consciousness. How amazing life has been; how magical the moments we've shared and experienced. Do we have to leave this someday? Is this the whisper we hear within?

The answer comes, "All that you have known and experienced of your special time here is going. Do you want to stay behind when all that you've experienced and known passes you by and dissolves into eternity to never be experienced again?"

This is when I realized that life is unique and our times are special and custom-made for us alone. Never again will there be a time like I experienced -- it was MY time and My life, custom-made and designed for me alone to share with a special group of others that I feel a connection to.

Generations come and go and it feels like they all have a separation of thoughts, feelings, and beliefs. The stage is the same, but the play is different. Life is a revolving door, a circular revolving stage, where several plays are presented. Each is a play, but they all cover different topics. I feel that our lives are very personal and an intimacy exists with each generation for the time they live. The issues, topics and experiences are all very personal to each generation.

With old age, it is easy to become depressed and disillusioned as we see opportunities and experiences slip away. Life as we see and experience it is for the young, those with the power to earn, and those with enough energy to accomplish it. For the old, there's the past to remember and the mystery of death to make peace with.

I hope as the years go by and I see my body lose its appeal and my hair falls out that I will never lose the awe and wonder of my heart. I hope I can still write poetry, share insights from my soul, and continue to marvel at and enjoy the love of my partner. I have made a pact with the universe to meet me halfway and share my thoughts, feelings, and insights from them. To do that, I can't stay in the past or live in hope of some imaginary future. It is NOW, inside me, in my heart, where I am aware that love is forever. Love never dies.

Dimensions of Living

Each of us carries within us an infinite capacity to experience life. What we call living now is not life. Life has a fullness and a depth to it and it expands with awareness, so that we can transcend the boundaries of our minds.

Today people live off borrowed ideas and embrace a system of living that is restrictive, preferential, and biased. Isolated from the real source of life, people today function robotically like machines. Life is always in the present moment and spontaneous, never planned or forced. It is living spontaneously through the heart and feelings.

You cannot plan a happy life or make past bad experiences go away, if you dwell on them. The mind, unlike the moment of NOW, reaches into the future for unfulfilled hope or judges the past as either good or bad. It cannot exist in the now or without time. It needs space and time as an arena for its purposes. The mind creates your world from the beliefs you accept as reality and then hypnotizes you into accepting that your reality is the only reality. It is selfish and blind to any other views outside its own.

We are what we believe and our beliefs are so strong and unconscious that we automatically function off them. This power to become what we believe is an ability of our consciousness to adapt and take many forms of existence, but it becomes a trap when we forget the core elements.

The mind is a gift, used to explore existence, but it quickly loses its way when the heart is not in charge. The mind is no longer is in touch with reality, but exists in imagination and fantasies as a way to fulfill itself. It will promise a temporary fix, but cannot guarantee lasting satisfaction.

To heal is to feel and to bring the creative aspect of the heart into the mind as a guide to proper self expression. You can dwell unconsciously and be a slave to others; you can choose to follow the ideas of others and be a carbon copy of them, or you can choose to explore yourself and follow the whispers of your heart. Then you will create naturally, according to your own special gifts and talents.

A satisfied life is one in which you express yourself fully from the heart, to heed those whispers that are uniquely your own and belong to no one else.

Big Business

I was talking this morning to my partner about the constant flow of credit card ads in the mail that try and get you to sign up. It dawned on me that big business relies on people signing up for more credit so eventually you will go belly up and they will own your wealth. I had never understood this before, but now it seemed so clear. While business promises you value, in the end, they are gunning for your wealth. They control the game and few people are aware of the principles behind the rules.

I am not against wealth and the wealthy, but I am making an observation that is true. There is a hieroglyph often seen in Egyptian paintings of a snake eating its tale. It suddenly occurred to me that life is like that snake -- life is eaten by death, just as the moon and night are eaten by the sun and daylight. It's a cycle of activity that is eternally changing, insuring that nothing is permanent in this world.

Yes, big business does manufacture certain means to make our physical lives better, but in the end and, at the root of their intentions, is your net worth. Everything is set up to gain it, and that's why they're *big business* -- and how they got *big*. They seduce you with ads, offers and, of course, lots of pretty girls with the hope of shutting down your brain and grabbing you by your financial testicles.

Their *generosity* is always hidden by a slight of hand written in small print when the purchase is made. It's sad that our wealth can't be gotten on honest grounds, but must come in the guise of some form of trickery. It often follows this saying of P.T. Barnum, "A sucker is born every minute."

It's a sad reality that we can't live without credit or big business or financial institutions, but I hope someday when an enlightened community exists, we'll find better ways to manage, accumulate and disperse wealth -- ways that don't hide intentions or cheat, but do offer a service to humanity in which all are winners -- not just big business.

I realize that humanity isn't ready for this, because the majority of us aren't ready to heal our doubt, fear, and low self esteem. The wealthy are creative and inspired in many ways to manifest what serves to make our world better, but it's the way in which they do it and their intensions that I question.

How can wealth be honorably gained when its basic principle is to make the other guy poor? Is this wealth, universal justice, or just the seed of greed and an excuse to be in control? Isn't greed a foolish waste of time where the ultimate winner of life is death and, like all things, death will gobble up greed?

The Ability to Receive

Perhaps you have wondered why those things we desire in life are so hard to come by or receive. It is one thing to desire an object, but entirely another to claim or receive it. One is of the imagination and the other is an awareness or *knowing*. One part is an activity of the mind and the other, a function of your connection to the source of life. Our deserving is short-cutted by our lack of self worth and the mind's capacity to distract us from our inner sense of worth.

It is one thing to know and receive, or manifest, and another to hunger after something. One is an idea that floats in our mind and thoughts enticing us and the other is an energy of knowing that compels us to act on guidance and *do something*. One is a deep recognition of our worth as manifested in an awareness of our connection to an abundant universe, sort of like having the keys to the kingdom, and the other is a hoping that we deserve or someday will be good enough to achieve our wants and desires.

Everything happens in its own time. It's not entirely up to us when we achieve a goal or a dream is manifested. Much of our time is spent waiting and wishing with a faint knowing that something good is going to happen *someday*.

Many promises of the soul are not manifested for years after first hearing a whisper, because it is up to us to grow into that which we seek and desire.

It is my experience that vision and wisdom are needed to lay the proper foundation for a dream to manifest properly. Without them, we can do great harm to ourselves and others. Great achievements and dreams are handled more properly when we have a certainty within that reveals to us that we are ready to handle them and will be guided to utilize them for ourselves and others.

You can spend all your life and energy seeking to get something or ways to try and control people and circumstances to satisfy your inner hungers, but until you learn to accept and receive, you will not know what you can handle, or know if you are ready to wisely manage great wealth, responsibility or power. Until you receive yourself in full awareness of all that you are and can know it is time to manifest your goal or dream, and you are ready for it, hoping is what you are left with and hoping does not have the guarantee of our awareness of what we deserve.

Laws are Meant to be Broken

I heard a long time ago that laws were meant to be broken and at that time, did not fully realize what this phrase meant. It seemed odd and even criminal to think such a thing. Time, seeing many things, along with experiences have led me to believe that this is a truth. It is not so easy to see for someone as young and naive as I was, but now I am convinced that it is necessary for man to evolve and become more aware.

Laws exist to control people's behavior and, while it may seem that certain behaviors are offensive and harmful to human life, who are we to say what should and should not be so. It is hard to say when laws were established, but it is certain that the idea of God has been used all along to influence people to do the will of those in power.

I feel pretty confident that those in power politically and religiously have used the idea of God and commandments for centuries to stay in power and rule over those too ignorant of the truth. Guilt is a powerful concept over a world that believes it is separated from a divine being, because of some wrong committed in a story. The Bible, Koran and other religious books are based on nothing more than what may amount to a fictional guilt.

Now, before you think that I am a criminal, an anarchist or a lawless person, I can tell you that I am not. I believe that the force of life, that which exists deep inside the soul of humanity, is good, positive, and knows how to love and be loved. It is also creative and respectful of all life. It does not need laws to be this way, because it is that way by its very nature. Laws in their way contribute to the so called evil in the world because they consider certain behaviors as absolutely bad. They label people black or white and leave little room for grey. They pass judgment and limit the scope of human experience which needs to learn by choice. They assume humanity has reached the pinnacle of its development. I don't think it has.

If mankind were done growing and evolving, then this hunger to know, inside us, would not be so great. Over the centuries, the churches and political parties have been making the same promises and NEVER keeping them. It is not because they don't want to, or don't try, it is because they can't. You cannot fix the problems of humanity with commandments, laws, religions, political parties, psychologists and presidents.

These ideas, organizations and people only serve to alienate people from themselves and their responsibility to learn, grow, evolve and become more aware. Laws don't fix problems, they create more problems, because they presume to tell a person, "If you do what I tell you, then you will be a better person."

Since when does obeying a law make you a better person or change you for the better? Laws are rooted in fear and established to control others who disagree with the majority. They presume, by saying, if a person only obeys the law he or she will be a better person, a whole person.

A person cannot become better by obeying a law, because a law has no power to regenerate, heal or enlighten. A law is simply an idea, a thought, or a dead concept that rigidly controls others and is slow to change when society's views broaden. History is full of situations where laws, commandments, and principles changed because they were proved false, limited, or suspicious in intent. If the ten commandments were from God and had the power to heal, then humanity would have been cured long ago by obeying them and regenerated from within.

Words have no power. Laws have no power to regenerate humanity. Only an awakened heart can reveal the truth and prove that laws are no longer needed.

Cosmic Sense of Humor

Inspiration can come at anytime and from any situation. I have often chuckled at the times when an inner voice shows me a truth, or gives a bit of insight about life to share. It shows me that a sense of humor exists in life and we shouldn't take ourselves so seriously.

This morning, as I was walking upstairs to the bathroom, I had an insight, one that I recognized as a whisper from my guides. It was alive and, like a seed, it wanted to blossom in my heart and mind and be shared with others. The only problem was, I had to use the toilet. So, with inspiration and insight blossoming, there I sat on the toilet. How spiritual that must appear to my guides -- talking to me while I'm on the crapper. I was afraid I might lose the inspiration through the reality of the moment.

Inspiration and insight can and often do happen when you're least expecting it. While the mind is distracted on some duty or idea, it's like a light bulb pops on above you and you know you have to give attention to it. You can feel it's important and true and you wonder where it'll lead you. You know it'll connect you to a place deep inside that recognizes truth and reality. I feel more whole at these times than any other -- except when I'm intimate with my partner, Cathy.

These moments feel like a part of us. More than random thoughts, they rise from somewhere deep as an extension of our being. We sense this, but we don't know how we do. Our minds can either function as a conduit for the insights or judge them, and the connection stops. Wherever mind is working, it is either serving the insights, interpreting them, or analyzing and dissecting them. Too much thought spoils the inspiration and dilutes the energy of the heart as they're revealed.

You never know when inspirations and whispers will come, but you realize they're meant to be shared. They can be given for you alone, but most likely, they should be shared as seeds for others to plant in the soil of their existence.

It's a joy to receive them and, no matter where I am, I'm glad they come. I'll share them as long as I breathe and my heart beats.

Dealing with Pain

When we don't know ourselves, it's hard to face hidden pain. Pain seems to overwhelm us. It feels as though it could even kill or devour us. Pain that's surfacing is often avoided by drugs, alcohol and other forms of addiction. It's like a merry-go-round and we think there's no escape. To cope, some will do almost anything and this is often worse than the pain itself.

Psychology, religion and mysticism have all evolved as ways to identify, face, and cope with pain but mostly on an intellectual level. The hope that's offered is one that may or may not come. While they can help us come to grips with pain, they don't stop it or make it go away. This is something we have to realize within ourselves. Pain will only leave, once we realize that an internal conflict is unwarranted or unnecessary. Pain comes when our actions and beliefs come into conflict -- when what we do or did isn't in harmony with what we were taught to believe. Pain exists because we have been taught to believe a right and wrong exists.

If we examine right and wrong, we find that over centuries, laws and religious commandments have been passed down without much scrutiny. We've all been led to believe that an unknown, invisible force, called God, is somewhere up there pulling our strings and he'll punish us for commandments we've broken. These commandments conflict with the reality of life's experiences and cause deep pain. Life is a conflict because our minds and hearts are at odds.

To kill someone is not wrong only because God said it is

wrong. Even in war, it hurts when someone dies, because a part of us dies, too. We are all connected. Our minds may tell us we come from a different culture or country, but our hearts and experience reveal that we're all the same and we want the same things. It's the realization that you and your enemy are similar that causes the guilt. Again, he was no different then you, felt as you did, and believed what you did. However, the label "enemy" stood in the way. No God needs to tell you this, your heart does.

There is no true forgiveness from the idea of a God that created hell and who sets levels of acceptance for us to get to heaven. Only the heart and an infinite universe that accepts and allows all things can solve the mystery of why things happen and how to deal with them.

The answer to tragedy in a person's life must come from beyond the mind and be realized in the heart with the help of a loving universe. Don't pray for forgiveness or look to God to make amends. Accept who you are. Accept what happened. Learn to accept the pain as a doorway to a greater understanding of life and *your self*. This experience can make a breakthrough to something more real and lasting, something that will go beyond ideologies, commandments, and even God. You come to the steps of reality and, in the end, you realize it does not matter, except in your mind.

I was riding in my car the other day and a whisper came to my awareness of the importance of writing. Something so simple and yet millions ignore it, mostly because of laziness and a lack of realization as to how important writing can be. There is also the fear that writing about it will reveal personal things people are afraid to face.

Creative writing and diary writing are very healing and can be therapeutic. They allow you to be in touch with yourself on a deeper level then just mind and reasoning. It is like a door to your feelings and unconscious is being unlocked and you have the opportunity to explore something about yourself. Sometimes it can be something which is hidden and buried.

Take any event in your life, past or present, and begin to write and explore it. Feel the emotions as you relive the experience. Remember, you are in control, so you can back away or avoid the feelings and emotions, but I encourage you to explore them. If you need to cry, then cry, but relive the experience. If you feel angry, then be angry, but explore the **roots** of the anger. See how it affects and has affected you, and realize that you alone are responsible for those feelings. They are affecting you alone. They are showing you the power your thoughts and feelings have had over your life.

Thoughts and feeling can cripple us in our development as a total person. When we believe something about ourselves and it is not bridged by an awareness of the truth, we can cripple and kill ourselves. By not facing self and the deep emotions of life, we prevent the healing passage into our awareness that gives the answer and provides the healing balm of truth. Do not push away the painful memories of the past. embrace them, face them with the same energy that you may have had to face enemy artillery or bullets. Realize that your life and happiness are important to you and others.

Understand that in the realm of your higher awareness, there is no medal or badge for having suffered. The scars you carry are your choices and the healing is also yours, if you embrace this opportunity to relive the past and release the fear that was repressed and not fully embraced when a tragic or scary event occurred.

Fear is a natural reaction when the mind feels it is losing control, and it is shocked into seeing that it can't be in charge of everything. Add to that the fact that it judges and holds many contradictions of beliefs, and you have a recipe for a mental train wreck.

Sudden trauma, combined with intense fear, makes us afraid that we will lose our life. This realization, rather than being faced and recognized as normal, is often pushed aside and buried. You see, the mind is proud and believes it can achieve a state of infinity, but it cannot. You will not take your current state of mind into eternity.

The question of life can't be answered, unless death is faced. It is death which gives meaning to life. It is death which brings the question of life's meaning into our consciousness.

If you have ever faced death, you know that the intensity of fear is like a cold steal rod being pushed into your brain. It paralyzes and shocks you into denial. It can also push you over the edge of mind into reality. Men often go into war with a sense of pride and confidence, only to be humbled and confused by the fear death brings. The price of glory is the wages of fear.

The Power of Writing

The universe does not judge us nor the choices we make. It allows us to experience whatever we choose. But there is a price for unconscious choices that are not based on truth about the higher nature of existence.

We feel pain when we make a lower choice. We hurt when we realize through experience that we made an ill advised decision. Sometimes we are too proud to admit we were naive and need to face it. You will never be able to explore the meaning of life, until you have faced the reality of death. Death brings the question of life into immediate attention.

Soldiers in combat often suffer for years over memories and experiences that are unresolved. They lie buried and unresolved within. Guilt is a big issue, as they felt they should have done more to save a life or prevent an experience from happening. Many things are out of control in combat and they often feel responsible for death cheating them or their brothers. It is a burden too great to bear for some. Death is life on steroids.

I remember watching a movie a few years ago called THE THIN RED LINE. It was about World War II and a group of soldiers facing a life or death situation. In the movie, you watched men face death, fear, confusion and anger. However, one soldier in the movie was different and most of the movie was taken from his point of narration. He seemed to see his experience of combat from a transcended place. He was not afraid, just aware of everything going on.

For some reason, he saw war as not a horrible and terrifying experience, but a drama that he had no control over. So, rather than give in to his fear and try to control his fate, he surrendered to whatever was going to happen.

Death strips us of our pride, our manliness, and our goals. It wipes out hopes and dreams and renders one totally helpless. It shocks the mind, because the mind cannot comprehend death. It sees it and fears it, but has no control over it. Death is in a realm beyond the mind's ability to grasp. The soldier was able to transcend his fear and see war and combat as a stage in which men faced their *self* and revealed who they were. In the end, he was led to make a choice between saving himself or another soldier. He chose to give his own life because he was aware that this point in time was where life had brought him and because he knew fear had no hold over his choice.

When we can die freely because we are aware life has brought us to a destination or a conclusion, fear has lost its grip on us and we surrender to it willingly. We do not question why or ask who we are. We do not doubt or criticize ourselves for our choices. We simply surrender to what is and accept our fate. It is time to let go of the past. You see, those of you who suffer, you have not let go. Still you hold on tightly to it because you have not sought the answers deep inside. What you dread is a gift to explore *self* and the meaning of life without judgment or condemnation. All it takes is courage and a willingness to learn.

Wishing the Darkness Away

Darkness affects all of us. It doesn't matter what age we are or how much money we have. Moments of fearful darkness, at times, wash over us and seem hell bent to overpower us with whispers of fear. Some wake at night with cold sweats. Others develop social phobias or anxiety attacks. Because the roots of darkness are unconscious, we seldom see the cause, till we have an experience and then we often shake in fear.

Darkness is an accumulation of repressed emotions, ideas, and experiences that we fail to face initially and they become buried within us. The mind can only accept so much, and when an experience is too horrible, it's pushed aside, as though it never happened at all. It goes into the body and the unconscious, where it waits and gestates.

Nothing in the universe evaporates and disappears forever. Everything goes *somewhere*. It goes to where it continues forever and evolves. The experiences and thoughts are energy. They have a mass, even though their weight may not seem like much.

In the unconscious, these negative charges, or experiences, are festering and seeking release, but it's prevented by the ego. The ego fears such a release, because it can lose its control over both the mind and the life of a person. The fear experienced in a phobia or anxiety attack (a spell of darkness) is mostly caused by the amnesia of having repressed the memories of related experiences over a lifetime. Like a volcano, the pain gets so severe in the unresolved subconscious that it threatens to erupt into the conscious.

The mind continually fights this and one is left with a paralyzed feeling of despair. Medication and therapy can help to alleviate these issues, but they only treat symptoms -- they're not a cure for the cause.

It's hard to feel fear and face it. The mind says to run and not let go of control, while inside it feels like something is going to die -- and you're not sure it isn't you. The normal reaction is to run or distract the mind into believing the pain is imaginary. Sometimes you can do this. Other times the pressure is too great and a breakdown is certain to occur.

Breakdowns happen when the contents of the subconscious become conscious and the mind cannot interpret or face events that participated the pain. The mind becomes horrified at what it senses from the unconscious and it shuts down. Emotions take over and cries of insanity seem to overcome one's self in waves of near madness. It's not pretty, nor is it pleasant. The mind feels it's in a thunderstorm and it can't see the sunlight for the clouds. It's the dark night of the soul.

Darkness is a resistance to things we judge as wrong. We give our self a message that something should not have happened or possibly, that we are at fault. In essence, it's judging or condemning our self psychologically over things we had little or no control over. It is judgment based on guilt and often unclear within us.

Conscience is the creation of religion and, while the Ten Commandments are great ideals, the reality is, we still have the freedom to choose our actions. A deeper question might be, where did we get the idea of judging ourselves for our actions?

Things happen in life that we can't control and it does no good to punish ourselves for them. This doesn't mean we shouldn't discern whether the effects of our actions are pleasant or painful. Our hearts know what's good and pleasant and peaceful for us. After the mind has broken down and its hold over us has washed back to sea, a curious thing happens. An almost peaceful and serene clarity arises. A heartfelt awareness is born after the dark confusion is washed away in bitter tears. What we felt as certain death and punishment melts into expanded clarity or knowing. The gift of darkness is the soil on which awareness of self grows. We can only discover our depth through our darkness. It's like lifting weights -- resistance builds strength.

The mind's inability to cope is the necessary resistance that causes the heart to open and the spirit to bring a deeper awareness and insight into our nature. The universe doesn't judge us, the mind does. When we can see our lives from the depth of our awareness, the pain of unresolved unconscious memories melts in light of our higher consciousness. Yes, those events happened and they hurt, but no one is condemning you ... but you. You realize you were a slave to your mind and your ego. You can't wish away pain and darkness, nor can you hide from them, but when you see them through the eyes of truth, both dissolve in your new consciousness. Peace is the result of acceptance, surrender and nonresistance.

The Universal Symbol of the Magic in Mankind

The symbol that you now see throughout my Facebook account and elsewhere is a representation of an inner energy or process of manifestation and transformation.

Before a person can manifest a new life, there must be an inner transformation of consciousness in which the old beliefs, perceptions and programming are removed by the emergence of new life. This life is in everyone and it is everywhere, but it cannot come into consciousness till we choose to question and investigate our beliefs and the experiences they have brought us, until now.

The six outer sides are representative of mankind. Six is recognized as the number of man. The eight triangles represent the numerous multidimensional facets within a human being that can be explored and discovered within.

The two facing pyramids mirror each other and reflect the manifestation of the inner realizations into the outer world. There is a saying: "As above, so below". Creation that begins in the formless and manifests into the world of matter, form and time.

The three sides of the triangles represent the basic trinity of existence and universal relationship of creation and manifestation. Heart, Mind and Universal Consciousness all working in harmony and with purpose. that purpose is the furtherance of life.

In essence, this is the process of magic and alchemy symbolically. Each person is capable of transforming their self when they dare to explore their feelings and emotions honestly and thoroughly. It is an ongoing process.

In the world before us it will be necessary for those who are awakening to reclaim the magic within them. To realize that their outer world is based on their inner one, to come to know and realize who they really are.

To the rational person the concept of magic seems childish and foreign to their consciousness, but to the aware person it is a sign of hope that there is a way out of the prison of their mind and into the freedom of their hearts.

Just as I was once told that the world was created with a heart, it will be reborn with that same heart. Collectively our hearts and the universal heart of consciousness will join together in a partnership that will create a better world than the one we find ourselves in now.

WHY?

What I am about to write, I cannot prove. It came about as a result of inner spiritual whispers and remembering a comment I read years ago from a friend's spiritual guide. It has to do with the beginning, our origins, and how we came to be. It all centers around the question of WHY.

Why is a perfectly normal reaction about something when we feel we don't know or are confused. In this context, however, we are talking about beings that were existing in a state of elevated awareness who were fully aware of who they were. Still WHY was asked, and an explosion resulted, an explosion of consciousness that trickled down into various forms of manifestation. The question of WHY, by its very nature, is almost an affront to that which is. It implies an unrest and a hunger to discover more. There is always a price to pay when you ask WHY.

The price, in this case, was the evolution of the mind. A being that knows *self* cannot question WHY, because they already know self. So, a fracturing has to occur, a break off from true knowing. An artificial existence was created, where mind and thought could explore, create, and try to discover the meaning of life or the existence of the universe.

The memory of our previous existence lived in our feelings for some time, but gradually as the mind became attached to thought, that memory faded and a series of digressions occurred, as what was once true to us became nothing more than a series of fables.

Guilt entered into our consciousness as we fought to return to the former state of innocence, but we could not remember our way back home. Our identity had shifted so far into our thoughts that we could not remember who we were in our feelings anymore. Caught by the mind's trap to keep itself in charge, guilt was created to seal the division between mind and heart. Guilt is the way the ego punishes us unconsciously so we will feel we are unworthy of existence or fullness of life. It keeps its power and place in us by making us feel we have done something wrong and we do not deserve to feel *right* again.

Condemnation grew over time as we lived with guilt and tried to make the best of the prison guilt placed us in. Forgetting the truth, we began to create stories of the fall of Adam and Eve, to explain as best as possible how our situation began. It was an attempt to keep in memory what the ego and mind could not know by experience anymore.

Mankind began to turn away from its knowing of existence and created false representations of reality in religion, politics and government. Trust within had eroded so far, that mankind felt lost and began to explore physical reality in an attempt to hopefully find a door or way back to our former state.

Parts of us wanted to die and, therefore, death was created by the mind and ego to prevent our return and keep us in bondage to this world. The will to control and power evolved from this as the ego, or mind, fought to stay in control, but deep inside, humanity still had a glimmer and a memory of what once was.

The further mankind evolved in mind and thought, the deeper the schism between feelings and mind became. It was not enough for guilt and condemnation to bridle the spirit of man; something else was needed to seal us to this world to forever forget our divine heritage. Fear was created upon the seeds of guilt and condemnation. The WHY that had begun the journey into matter and could not find the answer had evolved to a point of desperation. In that desperation, it realized one thing -- it would never find the answer this way. It had reached a point where it knew it could go no further.

Amnesia evolved out of the fear, as mind could not tolerate fear and ego was too proud to admit it. Ego and Mind decided to forget, repress or bury what WHY had discovered and began to invent ways to cope.

Coping is what man has done for thousands of years and beyond. Fear, guilt and condemnation created an illusion in the mind and ego of mankind, and what has evolved is a world still searching for the soul it lost somewhere back in eternity. People have become as machines and robots to systems and ideas. Still deep inside, a hunger still lurks. The question that started it all is still there and so is the distant memory of something more ... the WHY.

The Next Step

I have been at this process of inner transformation for a long time -- ever since a breakdown in 1971, when I had my first contact with the universe. I have read almost all the books on trans-personal psychology, magic, enlightenment and self help. While they all offered excellent insights, I have found that not every shoe fits all feet.

In the beginning, we all seek advice and inspiration from people we think know. We read books, listen to tapes and such. We may join churches or groups that seek to explore what we are searching for.

Sooner or later, the politics, personal differences, and boredom set in and we are off again on another search. If we are lucky, we meet some genuine enlightened beings on our way and they can be helpful to us on ours, but they, too, will eventually fail to live up to our expectations in some way and we also leave them in time.

Finally, we are left to our own devices and this is what we have been told all along, but feared to accept, because we don't trust ourselves or life at this point. We do not understand the connection between mind, experiences and reality. Because we are cut off from reality by our minds, we struggle in the dark and fall over all the furniture.

Over time and many trials we begin to look closely at ourselves and realize we are the only ones that can solve our problems. The priests, psychologists and self-help gurus can talk about our feelings, help us to accept them, but only we can transform them. That transformation can only occur when we accept full responsibility for our thoughts, feelings and actions. This is the first step to reclaim your identity and empower you to see how reality and you co-exist.

The encounter with reality is very subtle at first. You may hear and see things, audio and video whispers. Sometimes you may feel you are going crazy, but unless there is a real psychological or medical problem, you settle down and learn to observe.

Nothing by chance happens in life and unless we fail to learn from our experiences -- and some do -- you will begin to realize you are going somewhere. There is a reason your world is so crazy and you are not like others. This can be very lonely, but you also discover that others are having similar experiences. The logical world of expectations is giving way to the chaotic world of our individual realities. Further, we are asked to question, explore, and delve into ourselves.

Little by little, the mind loses its grip on us and we reach a place where we listen to our feelings and awareness. At first it is challenging because our mind says it can't be real. We ask, did I really hear that? Did I see that? Why did I have that dream? All of it is so contrary to what we have been doing for years.

In our desire to understand these happenings, we misread them or fail to clearly understand their meaning and intent. Still we can't ignore them because the old reasoning and thinking does not hold true anymore for us. We are in a new land, a magical, liberating, mysterious and confusing land at first. We have to unlearn and begin to feel. Learn to not trust our mind and judgment and experiment with our new awareness and realizations. To be aware does not mean you stop learning, growing or stumbling along.

The next step for me is to discover in my awareness those gifts, talents, and abilities that serve to bond me to a vibrant and living universe and to share these realizations with those who wonder what's next. Evolution does not mean to acquire more refined knowledge and experiences that say we have arrived. It is an awakening to ourselves, a clarification of our identities, a realization that we do know more than we thought and believed. We learn we are capable of leaving our limited minds and experiencing dimensions within ourselves that answer the age old question of ... WHO AM I?

God or Universe, Which is it?

Depending on what part of the world you come from, this is a big question and debated often. In the West you are asked to believe in a God that we can't see, know or hold an actual two-way conversation with. This is simple, efficient, but is it a relationship or a blind believing of ideas that we accept as children without question? Does it satisfy the heart to know this or merely appease the mind and its futile search for fulfillment?

Much of what is concocted in the west about God is imagination and conjecture. It has no basis in reality. What alive person has ever seen heaven, God, or another dimension and can prove their existence to others? This is not to say that people don't have spiritual experiences, but they are so individual and personal, you can't give them to others. So people afraid of self learning and discovery accept these stories and suffer because beliefs can't cure the separation between ideas and reality. Reality can be and must be encountered individually.

In the East, for the most part, there is no belief in God, but an awareness that something exists and connects us to each other and existence. It is not an idea, but a feeling, an awareness that unity, or oneness, is the nature of life. This did not come from ideas alone, but experiences over centuries of people who did not belong to churches, follow societies, or surrender to a master.

Meditation and enlightenment are paths, or tools, that are taught in eastern countries and meant to help the seeker to be in touch with their feelings and desires. The responsibility for a person's growth is on them and not based on ideas or a group or a master.

I realize that in the east, much of what has been passed down through the ages has turned into beliefs that people follow. However, if they are really listening and working inwardly, they realize that their enlightenment is a personal thing, not a commodity that can be sold by anyone.

In the final analysis, God is a word. The Universe is a physical phenomena, and Awareness is the key that unlocks us and allows us to experience both as ONE thing. Definitions divide, Awareness awakens and unifies -- it unifies the mind and heart and reveals a truth that can't be spoken easily.

How to Access the Magic

I'm sure there are all kinds of looks on your faces when you read my blog and I mention the word *magic*. For some, the look could be saying, "Is this guy kidding?" or, "What has this guy been smoking?" Others may feel a child-like wonder well up inside and they remember when they were kids and had hopes of doing the impossible. It's a term that sparks both hope and dismay.

Others will see it as creative ability, expression, or art, and identify it with their own inspiration. They can only tell you that, for some reason, they sense or feel a compulsion to manifest with paper, pen, or brush certain impulses and images that come to them in their consciousness. Where these impulses come from they may not be sure, but they usually find great pleasure and joy in sharing these gifts with others. Musicians and singers also fall into this class as well as poets.

If you ask them how they do this, most of the time they can't tell you. Mostly, it's automatic, or it happens when it happens. One thing is for sure, it does not usually happen on command. Most of the time it happens when you least expect it. Respect of the magic and a willingness to be available to it is important.

You can disrespect or ignore these impulses and they will lessen or even go away. This would be tragic, because nothing reminds us more of the eternal or existence of a greater power than when we create or express our vision. It is a link to what I call the *magic*. We feel less alone and more worthy when we are connected and can express a deep insight. It means we have a purpose and a reason for *being*.

My understanding is that the magic is everywhere. It is in everything. It waits for us to become aware of it and surrender to its presence in us. Some people feel that it would be nice to have a power to control others or force things to happen at will. They fear that who they think they are is not enough to be happy or successful in this life. Motivated by fear and a deep lack of self-worth, they seek to misuse the power of their magical connection and usually end up in deep mental turmoil and confusion. They do not understand that you cannot control the magic, you can only surrender to it and allow it to flow through you and bring new life, to you and to others.

You do not have to pray or beg for the magic. No higher authority sits in judgment over you. These ideas are what keep a distance between people and their magical nature. It is a conspiracy between those who want to control others and those who feel powerless and want others to guide and control their lives. Both have been a recipe for disaster for centuries.

You do not need a King, a Queen or a President to run your life or hypocrites to create laws that protect their interests and keep the masses in check. The conspiracies of fear and ignorance have served well those who have sought to gain over others and not give of their best to mankind.

Magic is what *you* are. It flows into and out of you from the universe. You do not need to buy it, seek it, or sacrifice for it. It waits for you to recognize and be aware of it -- to rejoin with it and feel it once again rush through you, showing you the possibilities and the promise of its presence.

It offers to guide you if you allow it, only working though you if you serve it for the greater good of all. The future is never set in stone and predictions are never absolute.

We are the Universe

Until this thought sinks deep into your awareness and lives, you will *never* discover the mystery of the universe or recognize your personal power. It is the denial of this truth which leads so many astray, seeking to become other than what they are, naturally, merely creating hollow images and lives built on the suggestions of others.

Faking it, they try and trick themselves into believing they are happy and powerful. Their self-worth is based on what they have accumulated, not what they actually *know* within. Separated from their true self, they travel in circles on an endless merry-go-round that temporarily satisfies the image, but not the soul.

You cannot enjoy fully what is not real: that which appeals to the mind, but not the heart. It isn't that we aren't all a part of the universe, because we are -- it's just that the awareness has been clouded by reason and logic. This disconnect leads to an outer *seeking* for something that is *already within us.*

To know oneself is to realize you lack nothing and that every event in life is guiding you perfectly to a further unfolding and recognition of your true identity. The universe wastes nothing. Even the baggage of our dark sides is fuel for a fire that purifies the separation and solidifies into our awareness the truth -- that we are one with all life. The church, the temple, the synagogue and the teacher or priest are all within our awareness. The Bible, Koran and the Gita are all alive in our awareness. Outside of your awareness, they are dead symbols with no power to heal or raise your awareness.

Life After Death

Isn't it odd that the world is full of religions that believe certain things and teach certain things about life after death, but none of them can prove it? Most religions rely on old stories, fables, and beliefs worn out over time. Still, people hunger to grasp for some sign that life after death exists.

It is sad to see so much of humanity groveling at the doors of churches, temples, and cathedrals that promise much but, in the end, deliver almost nothing. Fear is still with us and, no matter how much you try to hypnotize yourself, program yourself, or trick yourself, it does not go away. Death is in the realm of what is beyond thought and emotion. It lurks in the mystery of existence. It stalks us or maybe it waits for us to surrender to it so that it can reveal its treasure.

To lose control is a terrifying experience for most people and death is the ultimate loss of control. The mind fears anything it cannot relate to, and it struggles to hold onto in times of crisis, confusion and despair. We know little of ourselves beyond the mind, and death seems to be an eternally illusive nemesis, our greatest opponent.

It is the focus on our reason, our thoughts and mind, which make death an opponent. It is our lack of awareness through feeling that keep us from understanding and appreciating that, without death, we could not exist and life would have very little meaning for us. Death in many cases drives us to great achievement, success and creativity.

Death is the doorman to the NOW. It brings us into reality and keeps us there. The person who is dying is deeply aware within. They have no future in this world and their memories can't go with them.

When you leave this world, your beliefs stay here. Death is an experience and an awareness and the truth of it can only be known by one who has passed through its gates. No religious person, organization or group can die for you or with you. You, alone, must experience its reality and what lies beyond.

Awareness is a gift within that we all have. Awareness is the eyes of our consciousness shining into the unknown and it is the friend of death. To be aware is to know that death is only a *word* and that you are forever in the eyes of your awareness.

The Poison of Pain

Pain is a reflection of not accepting who we are and allowing our minds to judge and define us. The mind scrutinizes selectively, but it cannot be totally discerning. It is 2D, whereas the heart and feelings are 3D.

You suffer most when you cannot control things or people the way you want to. Your mind says you should be able to, but reality says otherwise. Your mind is born in the pain of separation from the total self.

Everything is given to you in life that you need at the right time. The mind says NOW. This lack of power to get what we want, when we want it, causes confusion. Our needs and the way we compare ourselves to others causes us to believe that we should have what they have NOW, and that we may even be more deserving than they are. It is this comparison to others and our lack of awareness and discernment of life that aggravate us and blind us to the wisdom found in waiting.

Life will provide everything for your good and growth, if you allow it. It will nourish and teach you, and prepare you for better things. If you listen to the pain and insist that your way is the only way to stop the pain, you might achieve this goal, but you will never satisfy the pain. The pain cannot be satisfied by anything other than to let it go and trust and accept your reality.

All of your life you may have been taught you have to fight for what you want, that you are in pain because you have been denied. The truth is, you are always in pain because you deny the deep self and its ability to provide what you need in its time.

Pain is always created when you run away from the reality of *self*. You have no pain when you are totally in acceptance of self. This true self only appears when your mind takes a back seat to the deeper reality that you are. Pain is the result of trying to become someone else, rather than to discover and allow your real self to emerge from within.

Trust and Power

Why can't we, or don't we, manifest our desires with ease and simplicity? Why is life so hard and at times it seems our simplest needs are unmet? Could it be that we are missing a truth or a reality about life and ourselves?

Take a minute and feel inside yourself. Become aware of all that you are and realize you feel alone. You may feel empty, you might be bitter and angry. A sense of being cutoff is felt from others and life. This territory is the borderline between you and eternity. It is the "I" of your ego that you are looking at.

The ego is an accumulation of thoughts, memories and programming. You and I have been programmed and hypnotized to accept reality in the same way others have for centuries. Our families, religions, governments and home towns have all conspired rather ignorantly to create a view of reality that is peculiar to their limited perceptions. These limitations and perceptions are not bad or evil, just incomplete.

The reason we do not trust ourselves or reclaim our power is that we have an incomplete awareness of who and what we are. The dividing line of the ego cuts off or separates us from the awareness of wholeness and perfect natural power -- power that works in harmony and conjunction with a balanced, natural universe without end.

Our minds cannot bridge ego, because the mind and ego are one and the same. We naturally identify with thoughts and assume they are reality. Our deepest fear is actually a suspicion that who we think we are is not real and something important is missing in our lives.

What is missing is a full awareness of our self, a deeper connection than just our minds. We are divided in our self-perception. We do not perceive or grasp anything totally as we are. We only see a part of it.

To totally trust, we must learn to not trust our thoughts, beliefs, and the training from our past. We must give up identifying with anything other than our self.

Life is a constant process of being stripped of illusions and various deaths that whittle away at the lies we have embraced. What we call tragedies and crises in our lives are actually the universe giving us self-liberation from choices that have no real hope of fulfilling us. What power we do have is generated by fear and manifests as incomplete choices that have their end in death.

You can bet that if you have made a choice and it does not come from your truth inside, someday it will end. What we call failure in life is a choice, or series of choices, not made in full awareness.

Lack of power equates to a lack of full trust in self or lack of awareness of the total self. You are the only one that can bring trust to your *self* and a sense of completion and power. Nothing outside you can do that. You must choose the path of inner awareness and be totally alive, totally present, and completely in the NOW.

We are either servants to the vision of the future that the universe wants with our higher natures or we are slaves to the limitations of the past generations, where only the few have power and control. It is our choice to decide, each of us individually.

There is no need for violent overthrows or destruction of life and property. We just need to realize who we are and create more complete solutions to life's challenges. This we will not do alone but in conjunction with, and the assistance of, a loving universe that we are all a part of.

You are not alone in your struggle to achieve fulfillment and meaning in your life. Even when you look outward from that fearful and alone ego, behind it, and beyond it, is the answer you seek and the completion of your journey.

The Search for Self

Life is more than a search for meaning. Life is a search for self. It is a desire to expand our awareness and to include missing aspects of ourselves that we have learned to fear.

Fears come from not accepting all the aspects of ourselves, especially the painful ones and the biggest fear comes from not allowing ourselves to become aware of more than our minds.

We are seldom more than memories and hopes. We live in the past and the future, but never in the full moment of our reality. The wall of our ego blinds us to the greater aspects of ourselves and only in dreams, drug experiences, or rare occurrences, do we dare to imagine that life is more than we think. We are self-limited and we suffer for it.

Fulfillment is not something to chase or win. It is something to realize inside. It is an awareness that nothing really matters more than to be fully present in ourselves at all times. Oddly enough, many spiritual disciplines, especially in the east, teach their disciples that the first step of any spiritual growth is to be aware. We should be conscious of our walking, eating, thinking and doing.

This first inward step is the door and the key to knowing the unseen aspects of our thoughts and feelings. We encounter them within the context of where they live and sometimes they bully us. We get to know and observe them, sense their power and learn to work with them and not fear them. To realize that they are a part of something vast inside us and not the only parts within us. Freedom begins with this step.

The Chain of Magic

I was thinking this morning how I was able to put together a class multi-reunion last September. What did I realize or learn that helped me to see it through? The following is a series of thoughts I realized and felt deeply. I want to share these with others who are facing life-changing choices. I hope this helps.

HOW TO MANIFEST A VISION OR THE CHAIN OF MAGIC:

1. Ask yourself, do I have a vision or is it an emotional whim? A vision is a deep feeling of certainty that you are following something bigger than yourself.

2. Am I willing to see things through till the end? Do I have the confidence that I can weather any storm and what I need will be provided, as it is needed? Do I have a sense that all situations are already taken care of?

3. Is my heart big enough to allow everyone to have their say, but to stick to my vision when my heart says not to waver, even if others disagree? Can I feel people's hearts and their true deep needs or wants?

4. Am I willing to step aside if the majority cannot or will not accept my leadership and vision? While it may seem that you are a dictator to some, the universe only works magic when hearts are unified. If agreement can't be reached by a group then a single soul must act. Great things can be done when hearts are unified.

5. It is never about control, power or achievement. It is

about surrender, service and giving your very best part to life and others for the good of all. Great strength comes from great vulnerability. Have the courage to be real and to put aside all notions of others or yourself and do not judge. Be real, be yourself, as you really are.

6. Fear is an imaginary wall that divides, separates, and keeps people apart. Love is the courage to risk being human and finding out that you are no different than anyone else inside. Outside, you may look different, but inside, the rich and poor are all the same. Our hearts need love, unity, and acceptance. Your magic is inside you and you have what it takes, but you will have to risk to reveal the best part of yourself.

7. When each person takes this courage and allows the magic to surface, then this world of self-interest will change to a world of self-service and manifest the true potential latent in all of humanity. It is not that far away. It happens slowly as hearts dare to open to each other and share the magic of life.

YOU ARE THE KEY TO A CHAIN OF EVENTS THAT THE WORLD AND UNIVERSE ARE WAITING TO SEE HAPPEN.

Our future and the future of our children will be created from either greed and self-interest, or a joyful cooperation like children playing together at noon on a school playground, having fun and knowing all is well.

WILL YOU BE THE NEXT LINK IN THE CHAIN OF MAGIC?

The Wall

There is a wall between us, and between our making real communication. Every day we hide behind this wall of self and ego, and we seldom allow ourselves to venture into no man's land to allow ourselves to establish real communication or communion with one another. This wall protects us from vulnerability and keeps us from feeling the pain we all carry inside us. The disappointments and sorrows of our life are hidden behind it. We feel somewhat protected there, but also alone and detached from others.

We yearn to love and be loved, but we fear rejection. We fear to face the mountain of emotion that has grown there and the humiliation of feeling human. We are a mess, because we carry our burden of life, a life that is hard to bear, and we have few outlets to allow the pressure to release, except in the tears we cry when we're alone at night and in our own private moments of despair. It is this failure to share feelings that is the root cause of most of life's pain and anguish.

Alone, we gestate and torture ourselves in a cauldron of guilt and self judgment. We have been taught to distrust ourselves and to fear the scrutiny of others. We are trapped within ourselves and feel there's no way out.

We seek freedom in a lifetime search through people and ideologies that promise salvation and often leave us even more bitter and letdown. We are not taught the real art of inner communication. We are not taught that feelings are the inner language of the soul and heart. We stop short of real communication because the language of the heart is not an alphabet, but a living, conscious awareness of deeper aspects of ourselves. This self is connected to something deeper, richer and more fulfilling than our minds. This self is total and not fragmented nor incomplete.

All of our walls crumble in the light of awareness. These walls are the construction of men, societies, religions, politics and laws and even from within our own families.

Awareness is a fragrance of our deep self and anchored in the source within us. It is a clarity that penetrates lies, deceptions, and falsehoods. It is the fruit of realizing what is deep inside us and what comes back to us is that we are to share our true nature with others.

This wall is simply an illusion that says you are not OK or that you have to be someone other than who are you are, where you are, to be complete. Do not seek to tear the wall down, but dare to peek from behind it or, better yet, dare to see what is hiding and allow your awareness to show you what is there. The wall can trick you into thinking you are safe, but only awareness can show you that you are connected to a vast and conscious universe that is always supporting you and willing to nurture you when you allow it.

To be aware is to be conscious of what and how you feel. This is the first step and the only step needed to dissolve the illusion of the wall. If you can stop your mind and *feel*, soon your awareness will begin to show you the true nature of your life and how that flowing with events is the only sane way to maintain a balance and retain our peace of mind. It is your choice, always, your choice to live with the Wall or to live in Awareness.

Our One Desire

Our one desire is to be whole. It is as simple as that. We want to feel alive totally, not partially. We want to be more than a brain. We want to reconnect with the mystery of life, to sense the flow of the magic every day. We yearn to do more than merely see things, smell things, or hear things. We desire to be in total awareness of and with life.

Our nature is to do more than just observe. We hunger to know, and to do, and to become. We sense that there is more to life than what we know, but we have forgotten how to get back there. We have lost our way and we suffer because we do everything incompletely. We have forgotten how to FEEL.

We live out of our bodies, but we don't know how to live in them or with them. We take our body for granted and even ignore it until it is too late. We seldom consider that our body is a doorway, a bridge, between this world and another, between the seen and the unseen. Feelings make this possible. They reunite us with the unseen side of our reality. Feelings complete the mystery and they channel the magic when it happens.

To be whole is to follow the heart, embrace the magic, and use the mind to sculpt our own reality. Our whole purpose is to live life as it was meant to be lived in freedom and in communion with eternity.

The Less the Desire, the More Aware you are

Life is full of desires. They crowd our mind and consume the majority of our thinking processes. Desires always promise us we will find happiness if we only achieve their calling. Days turn into months and months into years and still they call us, but seldom deliver their promise.

We spend tremendous energy to achieve our desires' beckoning and many hours planning how to control things to make these desires ours. Still, they seem out of reach and, as the years go by, we feel frustrated and disappointed by their lack of presence in our lives.

Years then turn into bitterness, and frustration accumulates and we forget the joy of hopes we had as youngsters. Life seems dull and dark and we shut down. Actually shutting down is a blessing. Giving up is a liberty. We realize that life, our life, is not totally in our hands and we can't always have what we want when we want it. We simply live and life unfolds before us. We either react to it, or we accept it and become more aware.

To be aware is to know that desire takes you away from your reality and your truth. It allows you to see beyond the fear that desire is hiding. It allows you to know that everything is provided for and it all comes in the right time for you.

A person who is obsessed with desire is filled with fear. They doubt they will ever have what they need. Most of the time, they don't really know what that is.

To be aware is to know what you need and how to find it. It is to accept that life is what it is and that it is perfect as it is and that everything comes in its own time. To be aware is to feel the deepest currents in your life; to sense a oneness between yourself and life itself; to know that you and your reality are always in perfect accord; that life is a mirror of what you believe and are aware of. It also is a mirror of what you fear and doubt. Do not desire, but become more aware. It will show you what you need to be -- happy, fulfilled and whole.

There is No place like Home

To reclaim your life you must become solid within, condensed, and clear, and aware of nothing else but YOU. No thoughts, idea's or plans should disturb you. You are simply aware that you are the center of the universe, but not in a selfish way.

You have come to give, to serve and to share. Feel life. It is full within you and bubbling over. You are directed by a force deep within you.

At times, you are not sure it is you, because it is not the old you, but a new you. You have become a being that carries the dreams and promises of a better life. You feel calm, relaxed and you simply know that this is the way life is meant to be.

You have come home and all is well within and without. As Dorothy said in The Wizard of Oz, "There is no place like home."

It is Our Fear

Fear exists because we do not trust our self, or know our self deeply enough to realize we are one with existence. This is caused by separation and the ignorance that exists in our minds. We look away from the real self to search the world for meaning. but we always come up empty. Nothing satisfies, and nothing fills the desire, lust, and hunger for more.

We burn out because we seek a ghost of ourselves that is not real and doesn't exist. Only inside do the answers become, clear, crisp and alive.

We see, because we know, not because we think. We are, because we are conscious, not because we think. Thinking is for looking outside at things, but never for seeing them as they truly are.

You can never have a true communication with another, until you have true communication within yourself first. Words are merely symbols of life, but they are not life itself.

Religion is merely a symbol for the divine, but it is not the divine itself. Fear exists because we are all trying to be what we are not and the fear is there to say, "Stop and go back", reconsider from where you came and who you are. Fear always causes us to bury ourselves in false illusions or brings us to the door of truth. Only then, can we see who we truly are and fear will leave. We realize that what we thought was an enemy was really a friend.

Give or Take

This is what we are here for: to give or to take. For the majority of people, taking is the way in which they see life. Their needs blind them to the gifts they carry inside. Feeling empty, they seek fulfillment in things outside themselves. They look to others to guide, teach and lead them into an uncertain future. It does not occur to them that those leaders know little more than they do about life and how to get to where they are supposed to go.

Still, like sheep, they follow and they suffer at the hands of ignorant leadership. It is only when a person dares to look inside that they begin to see they have something to offer. It does not matter what that is unless they share it with others.

Too many people feel that they are not good enough to share or worthy enough to create. They hide their gifts and never allow themselves to nourish or be nourished by others. It is a world in which little things do matter. If it was not for the little things shared or given, more unhappiness than exists would be experienced. It is a truth that we are all needed.

We all need to give and share our heart gifts with others. This is the fuel that keeps life going, keeps it interesting, and shows its connection in unity and purpose. We have a choice, to give or take. What do you choose to give to life? What have you come to share?

Always Looking

WE are NEVER satisfied! No matter what we get in life, soon we desire more, be it a thing, a person, or an experience.

We may tell ourselves that what we have is enough, but in truth it never is. Each time something new happens, we hope to hold it and never let it escape us, but it does.

Life is a coming and going. In time, it is never stagnant, but it is the desire of our minds to hold onto what it cannot that seems to create a stagnant perception.

But change is always happening to us. We fear to admit this to ourselves. We push the thought away that we could lose a job, a partner, a home, a friend, or even our life. We don't wish to consider it. It never occurs to us that this is a natural part of life. Because we are unaware of why it is happening, we avoid considering any perceptions about it. We want it to go away.

It never occurs to us that this lack of satisfaction is a sign of a deep hunger for more life and experience. It actually is a signature of our eternal self. We always hunger to know more and be more, but realizing it is something else. We seem to only know what is outside us and pay little attention to that which is within us.

Love is a process of two seemingly opposite or different forces surrendering to the possibility of a third force that brings unity. It is this surrender that breaks the veil and opens the mystery. The magical flow is this energy.

Nothing in this world lasts forever, because it is created in the mind and lacks the balance of its opposing energy which is eternal heart. The universe is alive, but to our minds it seems stagnant. Science knows differently, the mystic feels it within.

Do not be afraid of changes or the loss of anything. It may be the loss that reveals to you the fact that nothing can be lost or that it was the thing you feared to lose that stood in the way of your deeper self discovery.

We are like drops of rain that sink deep into the earth to nourish it and we are drops of water that dissolve into the ocean of life and become one again. Separation exists because we IDENTIFY with our minds, thoughts, ideas of self, and do not often encounter our inner SELF.

Emptiness

Have you ever felt deeply alone, without purpose or guidance? Have you ever been lost in mind or heart? Have you ever felt stuck or like you were going nowhere fast? Have you ever been at the end of your rope? Do you ever feel like your life has no meaning anymore?

This, oddly enough, is a good place to be. These places scare us, confuse us, disturb us, but ultimately, they show us how little we know about us.

We are okay, as long as we can function on the outside and act like other "normal" human beings -- robots and slaves to cultural programming. But when we encounter our own mystery, we freeze and cry and avoid the pain.

The ego does not like being reminded that it has limits. You can fool yourself only so long, that life is where it's all at, but suddenly, something reminds you that it is not. A death, an unexpected crisis or failure, cause you to doubt yourself and the life you are living. You feel helpless, or to be more accurate, your ego feels helpless. The ego can't see beyond the confusion, anger, pain or doubt. It wants to, but it can't. It has limits. It only exists and functions on the plane of thought, mind, and outer sensation. It does not go deep enough, far enough within to satisfy our need to know why.

We all live with a sense of being pulled along, while something is left behind. Something is hidden inside us. It is a knowing, a realization, or an experience that can put us back together, but we are afraid. We come to the door at times and freeze. We develop addictions to forget the door, the pain or doubt. Still it calls us.

As we get older and see death more closely, we can't avoid it and we know it. Someday we WILL pass through that door and maybe never return.

The world is full of ideas about God, the afterlife, and spirituality, but until we experience this reality, we are just living on hearsay. We are mostly believers that know nothing.

The emptiness is our friend. It brings us to the door of self encounter. It reminds us how lost we feel and separate and angry. It helps us to dissolve the illusions of this world and see life more deeply and clearly. If only we could surrender to it, allow it to saturate and cleanse us. It would reveal something more real and eternal in us. It would connect us with that which we are, and what our minds seek. We would be home and our search would be over.

Cycles of Living

Life is full of cycles, and polarities or opposites. We never stay on the mountain without an occasional trip to the valley. This fluctuation helps us to gain perspective on things, so to more fully understand an area of life.

Without extremes, life would become boring and eventually miserable. The reason for this is, our life reaches beyond our minds, experiences and perspectives. We are not just what we think, but more accurately, we are what we feel.

We are a consciousness that extends beyond time and space. Our minds assist us in dealing with our material reality, but minds are helpless to assist us in understanding the depth of our awareness. Only by being tossed beyond our minds do we regain the necessary insight into our true nature and existence itself. It is the desire to hold onto the past, a person, or a place that creates the pain of living.

When you learn to accept the cycles of life and allow the dark moments, moods, and situations to come without resistance, you will find that naturally you rise with a deeper insight into the nature of yourself, life and the experience you went through.

It is our nature to know, but not the knowing of books and education. Knowing the self is the door to truth and that truth is something the mind does not contain.

What is a Dark Moment

Death and change are often associated with dark moments. Depression is a long dark moment. We resist them all. We fear them all. They detach us from day to day living and, at times, they seem to doom us to continuous despair.

Seldom do we dare to look deeper into these screaming voices of pain. They remind us we are out of control, and nothing scares us more than the realization that we are not in control.

Life has to remind us that it has two sides, one side that we try to control, and the other side that we can't control. It is the mind's inability to control through understanding that causes fear -- and fear is the root of depression.

True understanding is not a function of the mind. Real understanding comes from INSIGHT, knowing what is true about a situation, person, or place. Insight is a function of awareness and awareness is the capacity to remember the limitless capacity of our consciousness to KNOW. We are more than death, more than changes and even more than depression. WE are LIFE.

Realist or Magician

The realist says, "Be practical, be normal, be like others. Don't change, keep the same schedule, the same relationships, even the same ideas and thoughts. Never embrace the unusual or bizarre, and never piss off those who count on you to give them support for their fragile images. Don't rock the boat, or follow the crowd! Someday, if you WORK REAL HARD, PARADISE will be there when you retire."

Do you hear these words, these promises? Do you believe them? Are you sure they will happen?

The realist always seeks to survive and at what cost is the denial of their personal feelings and needs? They are slaves to the ideas and systems of others. They carry a weight all their lives, the weight of self denial. They are filled with guilt from those who understand that it is easy to manipulate a person who lives in fear and needs help.

A person that has not learned to value *self* and question all the ideas they have been fed do NOT have a sense of self, only a self that is manipulated and controlled to serve others needs, desires and wants. A realist does not see anything special in themselves. They only deny their self and do what others feel is necessary and important. They are slaves to others who say THEY KNOW TRUTH, GOD, or REALITY.

A realist is beaten down by opinions, beliefs, ideas and people who are just as scared as they are, but who present themselves as knowing.

If I was to write a book, it would be called, "GREAT LIES WE LIVE BY". There are so many. They have existed a long time and they have made this world a hell for millions.

The dreamer, the magician, and the visionary feel that something better exists, something beyond the mind and what is seen. They have hope of a better tomorrow, but may not know how it can manifest. They walk the line between reality and illusion and they dare to seek truth on their terms.

No man is their GOD, PROPHET or SAVIOR. They often walk alone. They seek a life based on the deepest expression of their heart with no compromise. They want the truth, but not interpreted by others. They feel life can be better and are compelled to make it so. They dare to express their truth no matter what others think or say. They know the mystery of life and love and are at peace most of the time. They realize that they are in the hands of a higher power and must follow those intuitions as they are given. Piece by piece, step by step, slowly they manifest THEIR DREAM, THEIR REALITY as they courageously follow their heart within.

Only by knowing the vision within can we express outwardly the power that comes from knowing our truth. Each truth is as different as each person is. No other person can interpret it for you, you have to go inside and find it. It is part of the magic which you alone can manifest. Your special place in time and existence. WHEN WILL you claim it?

Poetry or Prose

I am debating today as to whether I want to write this as a poem, or in prose. I was in meditation this morning and as sometimes is the case, I became aware of my reality within. I could see my mind and feel the essence of me right along with it. It was like standing in between two rooms, in a doorway that enters both, one going outside and the other inside.

I realize the mind is for survival in this world and the heart, or feelings, are my true deep nature. I can see that the mind is a reflection, but not the full essence of me. The mind without the heart is only half alive. The mind can mimic the heart, but it never quite is up to the task. It lacks something essential. That *something* is beyond description. It is part mind and part heart, but even more than both. It is called many things: Light, God, Soul and various other terms, but they all miss the true nature of its essence.

One thing that occurred to me is that what we seek in words, definitions, and phrases is never able to capture the true essence of what we are trying to say. In other words, the word *love* is not the feeling of love, nor your name, who you really are.

In that silence, it became clear to me that what I have sought all my life, I already was. I am that which I seek. It is through this door that we realize the magic. When heart and mind surrender to this essence, we are magic and life has a bliss to it that colors all we do, say and feel. It allows us to create and manifest our dreams. Things and situations that were once difficult or blocked, simply open.

There is no hindrance to the dreams we have in our lives, except the one we create by trying to be more than what we are. If we accept ourselves totally, we can't help but live fully, because we create each moment of our life according to the level of awareness we possess of our self. It is always in our hands to move beyond limitation, pain and suffering. What is your choice today?

Trust is a Must

Inside us is a deep trust of consciousness. Our breath, our heartbeat, the flow of blood through our bodies, the impulses of energy from our brains to every cell in our bodies, the ability to move our muscles and walk and talk, all happen without any conscious effort. Deep inside, we trust, believe and accept without judgment, criticism or doubt that we are and we have a right to be, and to express ourselves.

Outside, it is a different matter. In the world, we struggle to know ourselves, to believe and to survive. We often fear the world, the people and even ourselves. Outside of our families and a few friends, it is hostile territory. It is me against them. The mind does this. It separates us from the heart, from the center of our being, from the very core of existence and from the unity of all things.

We feel separate and cut off, because we are distancing ourselves from the center of our being. We move away from the awareness of our hearts and souls to the ability of our minds to think, analyze and dissect. Because of this, we lose touch with reality, the REAL REALITY, and we are caught in the illusion our minds have created for us. We get lost in the doing and we forget the being. It is not wrong to be caught in the doing, but when we are separate from the being, we lose perspective, we feel the doing is all that matters or that the doing is all there is. This creates the feeling that something is missing, an emptiness or an angst. It is though we are fighting against something and we don't know exactly what it is.

Could it be, we are fighting against ourselves, our true nature and existence itself? Does it not say that a house divided against itself must fall?

To trust, you have to be deeply anchored in existence and yourself. Only then can you see the continuity of your day to day life in the context of something bigger than your mind.

The Path. What Path?

If you are looking for a single answer to the path of your fulfillment, then you don't understand the universe or your heart.

Many people seek a WAY or a particular path to reach fulfillment in life. THERE IS NO WAY OR SINGULAR PATH. Only the intuits of the heart leading you forward towards fulfillment as you are ready to feel them.

The universe is NOT a religion, NOT a church, NOT an organization at all, but a living, creating and evolving conscious energy. We are that energy. We don't need to worship it, sacrifice to it or (pardon the expression) KISS ITS ASS.

If you already are that which you seek, then why would you try to be other then what you are? If there is one great hurdle to your spiritual unfolding. it is the IDEA of God , which exists for many of us, an IDEA we have borrowed. This has been patterned after the idea of an earthly father or a false concept that male energy is superior to female energy.

Each in balance is perfect. Out of balance, they distort reality. You cannot heal, if you don't feel. If you want control, you will lose your soul. Only through awareness do you find a balance of both. Only through acceptance do you find peace and a chance to achieve harmony with your life. Life simply is manifesting itself without our help, without our need to control or manage it.

But our fears tell us otherwise. Fears are outside the realm of reality, and fears are mind-created and man-created. They steal the moment and take you into the past or into the future, but they never take you into the reality of who you are in that moment. It is that reality in the moment that is called *home* or the *path*.

The Magic is YOUR life, Fully Lived

Do you have YOUR life? Do you live YOUR life fully? Do you know what it means to have a life? Interesting questions, aren't they? I am sure that you have heard this all before and wondered what it means.

To have a life is to be in touch with the force of existence itself. There is no go-between, no outer authority. There's no one to ask what to do or where to go. No one but you and a connection to the deep center within yourself. A trust is found there and a confidence to believe that you have every right to create and manifest your vision.

This vision is not actually yours, but a shared vision that you receive from existence. You are a co-creator with life, a partner with existence. You share in the creation of the future. You feel worthy and at peace because you realize that you are a part of something vast and beautiful. You are HOME!

Anything we create that does not come from this center inside us is artificial, hollow and eventually dies. It may satisfy the mind for awhile, but it never reaches the heart or touches the hearts of others. Energy can be manipulated from the outside, science does it all the time, but look at the results. Energy that rises from the heart, or inside, is more comprehensive, full and lively. It nourishes and feeds other hearts. It lasts! Great art, writing, and creations last beyond their time. They give something back to humanity that says, you are so much more then you imagine. When will you begin the journey to claim back your life from the dust of false hopes and dreams??

Trust of Self

The magic cannot work through you, unless you trust your *self*. The reason for this is that you *are* the magic. For those who believe in a power outside the self, the magic will always seem beyond your reach. They hope for a better life or someday to control their existence. It is always a matter of not deserving or not being good enough or having enough faith or belief. They are forever caught in a merry go round of self doubt, torture and lack of worth.

To trust yourself, you have to know yourself and your real relationship to existence. Beliefs cannot give this trust. You do not have to believe, if you know. Beliefs are of no use to a person that knows.

In most cases, beliefs are the reason you don't know. They are a crutch that you lean on, because you fear you are not good enough or worthy enough to know.

Why do you feel unworthy? Who told you that you are not good enough? Who says that you are not perfect as you are, with flaws included? These are the questions you must ask to get clarity on why life seems to be such a struggle. Life can only be a struggle when you are still struggling within yourself as to who you are and what your real relationship to existence is. Know yourself is the path. Belief is not required.

The Magic Waits Patiently

It is there, can you FEEL it? It's there, deep inside you, beyond all thought, emotion and sense. Silently, it waits for you to remember, to see that it is there and always has been. The knower, the seer, the eternal you, is caught in the illusion of mind we think and seldom feel. We seek what can't be taught, learned or borrowed from another. It peeks out at times to remind us when we feel, or are inspired or creative. It reminds us that a fullness exists within us if we would only allow it.

How can you search for that which you already are? How can you find that which is not hidden? A riddle is meant to perplex the mind and cause you to go beyond it to discover a deeper, truer part of your self that lives in forever. It is meant to awaken you from your sleep, so that you can see and know and become.

The World Supports Creative Feeling or Vision

It is through creativity that we evolve and build our future. It is through individual vision that we manifest our desires. Without vision, mankind would continually run in circles. It would stagnate and eventually die for lack of newness and boredom.

If there is one thing lacking in humanity at this time, it is vision and the power to manifest our dreams into reality. We are never lacking in talk, debate, discussion, or criticism, but when it comes to actually making something happen, we often lack vision.

Vision is the voice of the future or creativity that isn't manifested. Some may call it God, but in reality, it is the ability to generate support, effort, materials, personnel and whatever it takes to make a vision a reality. It is the energy of existence, the magic saying YES to our desire to serve and inspire humanity through some effort or cause.

We work hand in hand with that force which moves the stars, makes rivers flow, and the sun to shine beyond the clouds of doubt and dismay. WE share in the purpose and higher intent of a magic that shines brighter and deeper than any sun in any galaxy of any part of this vast universe.

Trust, the Key to the Heart

If we don't have trust in ourselves, in life and others, then we feel cut off, abandoned and we feel that life is against our needs, hopes and desires. I am not talking about common trust, but something far deeper -- a basic and fundamental trust in the integrity of our connection in consciousness to all that is. It's knowing that you are part of this universal whole.

Most of us have limited trust or a trust with conditions, but this kind of trust will not weather a storm of doubt or an apparent betrayal. It does not see deep enough or far enough into the purposes of the magic.

Total, absolute trust or surrender is the way we melt into our deepest nature, the magic or love. At some point in our lives we all need to open and trust and share our common humanness and realize we are all the same. We may look different, sound different or feel different, but human needs, desires, wants and problems are universal.

To trust is to risk rejection but it's also the way to a deeper love of self and others. It is a glue that binds us all and supports our common need for love. The world and your life are seen from a different place when you view them with your heart.

About the Author

I was born Roman Catholic, became a fundamentalist minister at the age of 21, and then in 1983 I was introduced into Astrology. Since that time I have lived life as it has unfolded and discovered that each experience and event was a planned lesson or doorway into a deeper awareness or understanding of life. Trusting life and accepting the experiences that it brings you is the only real religion and offers us awareness when we do not shift the responsibility for our feelings onto others.

I offer astrology readings for those who are seeking insight into experiences that may be troubling their lives and my website, Magic Man's Universe is for anyone seeking deeper insight into Awareness and the unfolding of their life through experiences.

Magic Man's Universe
http://www.magicmansuniverse.com

www.ingramcontent.com/pod-product-compliance
Lightning Source LLC
Chambersburg PA
CBHW071009040426
42443CB00007B/730